A Summoning of Stones

THE MACMILLAN COMPANY
NEW YORK · CHICAGO
DALLAS · ATLANTA · SAN FRANCISCO

THE MACMILLAN COMPANY
OF CANADA, LIMITED
TORONTO

A Summoning of Stones

... to call the stones themselves to their ideal places, and
enchant the very substance and skeleton of the world.

SANTAYANA

ANTHONY HECHT

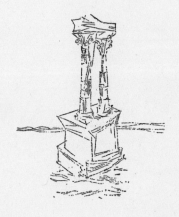

1954

THE MACMILLAN COMPANY · NEW YORK

To Roger

Contents

A Summoning of Stones

Double Sonnet

I recall everything, but more than all,
Words being nothing now, an ease that ever
Remembers her to my unfailing fever,
How she came forward to me, letting fall
Lamplight upon her dress till every small
Motion made visible seemed no mere endeavor
Of body to articulate its offer,
But more a grace won by the way from all
Striving in what is difficult, from all
Losses, so that she moved but to discover
A practice of the blood, as the gulls hover,
Winged with their life, above the harbor wall,
Tracing inflected silence in the tall
Air with a tilt of mastery and quiver
Against the light, as the light fell to favor
Her coming forth; this chiefly I recall.

It is a part of pride, guiding the hand
At the piano in the splash and passage
Of sacred dolphins, making numbers human
By sheer extravagance that can command
Pythagorean heavens to spell their message
Of some unlooked-for peace, out of the common;
Taking no thought at all that man and woman,
Lost in the trance of lamplight, felt the presage
Of the unbidden terror and bone hand
Of gracelessness, and the unspoken omen
That yet shall render all, by its first usage,
Speechless, inept, and totally unmanned.

3   201414

La Condition Botanique

Romans, rheumatic, gouty, came
  To bathe in Ischian springs where water steamed,
Puffed and enlarged their bold imperial thoughts, and which
Later Madame Curie declared to be so rich
  In radioactive content as she deemed
    Should win them everlasting fame.

Scattered throughout their ice and snow
  The Finns have built airtight cabins of log
Where they may lie, limp and entranced by the sedative purr
Of steam pipes, or torment themselves with flails of fir
  To stimulate the blood, and swill down grog,
    Setting the particles aglow.

Similarly the Turks, but know
  Nothing of the more delicate thin sweat
Of plants, breathing their scented oxygen upon
Brooklyn's botanical gardens, roofed with glass and run
  So to the pleasure of each leafy pet,
    Manured, addressed in Latin, so

To its thermostatic happiness—
  Spreading its green and innocence to the ground
Where pipes, like Satan masquerading as the snake,
Coil and uncoil their frightful liquid length, and make
  Gurglings of love mixed with a rumbling sound
    Of sharp intestinal distress—

So to its pleasure, as I said,
  That each particular vegetable may thrive,
Early and late, as in the lot first given Man,
Sans interruption, as when Universal Pan
  Led on the Eternal Spring. The spears of chive,
    The sensitive plant, showing its dread,

The Mexican flytrap, that can knit
Its quilled jaws pitilessly, and would hurt
A fly with pleasure, leading Riley's life in bed
Of peat moss and of chemicals, and is thoughtfully fed
Flies for the entrée, flies for the dessert,
Fruit flies for fruit, and all of it

Administered as by a wife—
Lilith our lady, patroness of plants,
Who sings, *Lullay myn lykyng, myn owyn dere derlyng,*
Madrigals nightly to the spiny stalk in sterling
Whole notes of admiration and romance—
This, then, is what is called The Life.

And we, like disinherited heirs,
Old Adams, can inspect the void estate
At visiting hours: the unconditional garden spot,
The effortless innocence preserved, for God knows what,
And think, as we depart by the toll gate:
No one has lived here these five thousand years.

Our world is turned on points, is whirled
On wheels, Tibetan prayer wheels, French verb wheels,
The toothy wheels of progress, the terrible torque
Insisting, and in the sky, even above New York
Rotate the marvelous four-fangled seals
Ezekiel saw. The mother-of-pearled

Home of the bachelor oyster lies
Fondled in fluent shifts of bile and lime
As sunlight strikes the water, and it is of our world,
And will appear to us sometime where the finger is curled
Between the frets upon a mandolin,
Fancy cigar boxes, and eyes

Of ceremonial masks; and all
The places where Kilroy inscribed his name,
For instance, the ladies' rest room in the Gare du Nord,
The iron rump of Buddha, whose hallowed, hollowed core
    Admitted tourists once but all the same
        Housed a machine gun, and let fall

    A killing fire from its eyes
During the war; and Polyphemus hurled
Tremendous rocks that stand today off Sicily's coast
Signed with the famous scrawl of our most traveled ghost;
    And all these various things are of our world.
        But what's become of Paradise?

    Ah, it is lodged in glass, survives
In Brooklyn, like a throwback, out of style,
Like an incomprehensible veteran of the Grand
Army of the Republic in the reviewing stand
    Who sees young men in a mud-colored file
        March to the summit of their lives,

    For glory, for their country, with the flag
Joining divergent stars of North and South
In one blue field of heaven, till they fall in blood
And are returned at last unto their native mud—
    The eyes weighed down with stones, the sometimes mouth
        Helpless to masticate or gag

    Its old inheritance of earth.
In the sweat of thy face shalt thou manage, said the Lord.
And we, old Adams, stare through the glass panes and wince,
Fearing to see the ancestral apple, pear, or quince,
    The delicacy of knowledge, the fleshed Word,
        The globe of wisdom that was worth

Our lives, or so our parents thought,
And turn away to strengthen our poor breath
And body, keep the flesh rosy with hopeful dreams,
Peach-colored, practical, to decorate the bones, with schemes
Of life insurance, Ice-Cream-After-Death,
Hormone injections, against the *mort'*

Saison, largely to babble praise
Of Simeon Pyrites, patron saint
Of our Fools' Paradise, whose glittering effigy
Shines in God's normal sunlight till the blind men see
Visions as permanent as artists paint:
The body's firm, nothing decays

Upon the heirloom set of bones
In their gavotte. Yet we look through the glass
Where green lies ageless under snow-stacked roofs in steam-
Fitted apartments, and reflect how bud and stem
Are wholly flesh, and the immaculate grass
Does without buttressing of bones.

In open field or public bed
With ultraviolet help, man hopes to learn
The leafy secret, pay his most outstanding debt
To God in the salt and honesty of his sweat,
And in his streaming face manly to earn
His daily and all-nourishing bread.

Fugue for One Voice

There are some people who would say that fish
Drown in the air; our element is so thin
It can't sustain the flourish of those gills.
This atmosphere, which is our medicine,
By its own delicacy kills.
You placed an orchid in a little dish
Of water. The pale orifice,
Prisoned in water, turned its petals out
As though desiring a kiss,
Or maybe in a comical grimace
Like the last gasping of a landed trout,
Absolute awe circled upon its face.

It was in this room we both jointly drowned.

With our immersion sea flowers came to bloom;
Borrowed by our imagination from
The tapestries of France, they filled the room
As they had once captured and filled the eye
With brilliant inflorescence of antique design
And climbed in whorls upon the crimson sky,
As though it were of brick, and they a vine.
And through their turning stems I saw
The hand-stitched image of a lady where she sat
Attended by small birds that made their caw,
And on her covered wrist,
Rendered in threads of umber and of blue,
A hooded falcon sat at rest.
There came before her in a curious hat
A gentleman of broad and burly stride
Who, with his thumb and index finger, held to view
The red meat of his heart
Which he had plucked out of his side,
And this was called, *The Offering of the Heart.*

This was not lavish if you bear in mind
That dynasties of fish, swimming before mankind,
Felt in the pressure of their element
What Leonardo charted in a brook:
How nature first declared for the baroque
In her design of water currents. Look,
Then, what our own weather can invent.
This was our coldest winter. It was no joke
That set those unbelievable tormented freaks
Howling and laughing on the finial point
Of churches. Wind opened their shrieks,
And snow worked out their eyeballs and their nails,
And drove, with missionary fury, to anoint
Abandoned cars with whiteness,
Until they mainly looked like stranded whales,
Whiter than legend, rotting in our streets.
Rioting air conspired to engrave
Outlandish thistles on the windowpane,
Rose without thorn, and prisoned all in ice,
Not more fantastic than the elaborate bloom
Of underwater plants.
                              They are the rich device
And emblem of our nature. See the wind behave
Like water. To drown is to remain
Entirely alive; it is to breathe.
Therefore believe the couple in your room
Nothing but natural.

Now it is spring, and the unclouded skies
Flatter the grass with sunlight. Thick indifferent blood
Rises again in the vast hearts of trees.
Upstream the fish are ripening for flies,
And flowers, that were buried underseas,
Being denied a refuge in the Ark
Against God's first, uncompromising Flood,
Blossom, beyond all reason, in the park.

Japan

It was a miniature country once
To my imagination; Home of the Short,
And also the academy of stunts
    Where acrobats are taught
  The famous secrets of the trade:
  To cycle in the big parade
While spinning plates upon their parasols,
Or somersaults that do not touch the ground,
    Or tossing seven balls
In Most Celestial Order round and round.

A child's quick sense of the ingenious stamped
All their invention: toys I used to get
At Christmastime, or the peculiar, cramped
    Look of their alphabet.
  Fragile and easily destroyed,
  Those little boats of celluloid
Driven by camphor round the bathroom sink,
And delicate the folded paper prize
    Which, dropped into a drink
Of water, grew up right before your eyes.

Now when we reached them it was with a sense
Sharpened for treachery compounding in their brains
Like mating weasels; our Intelligence
    Said: The Black Dragon reigns
  Secretly under yellow skin,
  Deeper than dyes of atabrine
And deadlier. The War Department said:
Remember you are Americans; forsake
    The wounded and the dead
At your own cost; remember Pearl and Wake.

And yet they bowed us in with ceremony,
Told us what brands of Sake were the best,
Explained their agriculture in a phony
    Dialect of the West,
  Meant vaguely to be understood
  As a shy sign of brotherhood
In the old human bondage to the facts
Of day-to-day existence. And like ants,
    Signaling tiny pacts
With their antennae, they would wave their hands.

At last we came to see them not as glib
Walkers of tightropes, worshipers of carp,
Nor yet a species out of Adam's rib
    Meant to preserve its warp
  In Cain's own image. They had learned
  That their tough eye-born goddess burned
Adoring fingers. They were very poor.
The holy mountain was not moved to speak.
    Wind at the paper door
Offered them snow out of its hollow peak.

Human endeavor clumsily betrays
Humanity. Their excrement served in this;
For, planting rice in water, they would raise
    Schistosomiasis
  Japonica, that enters through
  The pores into the avenue
And orbit of the blood, where it may foil
The heart and kill, or settle in the brain.
    This fruit of their nightsoil
Thrives in the skull, where it is called insane.

Now the quaint early image of Japan
That was so charming to me as a child
Seems like a bright design upon a fan,
    Of water rushing wild
    On rocks that can be folded up,
    A river which the wrist can stop
With a neat flip, revealing merely sticks
And silk of what had been a fan before,
    And like such winning tricks,
It shall be buried in excelsior.

Divisions upon a Ground

I

My demoiselle, the cats are in the street,
Making a shrill cantata to their kind,
Accomplishing their furry, vigorous feat,
And I observe you shiver at it. You
Would rather have their little guts preserved
In the sweet excellence of a string quartet.
But, speaking for myself, I do not mind
This boisterous endeavor; it can do
Miracles for a lady who's unnerved
By the rude leanings of a family pet.

II

What Argus could not see was not worth seeing.
The fishy slime of his one hundred eyes
Shimmered all over his entire being
To lubricate his vision. A Voyeur
Of the first order, he would hardly blench
At the fine calculations of your dress.
Doubtless the moonlight or the liquor lies
Somewhere beneath this visible *bonheur,*
Yet I would freely translate from the French
The labials of such fleet happiness.

III

"If youth were all, our plush minority
Would lack no instrument to trick it out;
All cloth would emphasize it; not a bee
Could lecture us in offices of bliss.
Then all the appetites, arranged in rows,
Would dance cotillions absolute as ice
In high decorum rather than in rout."
He answered her, "Youth wants no emphasis,
But in extravagance of nature shows
A rigor more demanding than precise."

"Pride is an illness rising out of pain,"
Said the ensnaffled Fiend who would not wince.
Does the neat corollary then obtain,
Humility comes burgeoning from pleasure?
Ah, masters, such a calculus is foul,
Of no more substance than a wasting cloud.
I cannot frame a logic to convince
Your honors of the urgent lawless measure
Of love, the which is neither fish nor fowl.
The meekest rise to tumble with the proud.

V

Goliath lies upon his back in Hell.
Out of his nostrils march a race of men,
Each with a little spear of hair; they yell,
"Attack the goat! O let us smite the goat!"
(An early German vision.) They are decked
With horns and beards and trappings of the brute
Capricorn, who remarked their origin.
Love, like a feather in a Roman throat,
Returned their suppers. They could not connect
Sentiment with a craving so acute.

VI

Those paragraphs most likely to arouse
Pear-shaped nuances to an ovoid brain,
Upstanding nipples under a sheer blouse,
Wink from the bold original, and keep
Their wicked parlance to confound the lewd
American, deftly obscured from sin
By the Fig-Leaf Edition of Montaigne.
But "summer nights were not devised for sleep,"
And who can cipher out, however shrewd,
The Man-in-the-Moon's microcephalic grin?

The Place of Pain in the Universe

Mixture of chloroform and oil of cloves
Swabbed with a wadded toothpick on the gums
Grants us its peace by slackening the thread
Of rich embroidered nerve spun in the head,
And to the weak and wretched jaw it comes
Lighter than manna and in sweeter loaves.

An old engraving pictures St. Jerome
Studying at his table, where a skull,
Crowned with a candle, streams cold tears of wax
On its bone features for the flesh it lacks,
Yet its white complement of teeth is full
While all its pain runs happily to loam.

Observe there is no easy moral here.
Having received their diet from the skies
The teeth remain, although they cannot bite,
And to perform inspection beyond sight
The empty sockets famish for their eyes.
The pain is lifelike in that waxwork tear.

As Plato Said

These public dances and other exercises of the young maidens naked, in the sight of the young men, were moreover incentives to marriage; and to use Plato's expression, drew them almost as necessarily by the attraction of love as a geometrical conclusion is drawn from the premises.

PLUTARCH

Although I do not not know your name, although
It was a silly dance you did with apple flowers
Bunched in your hands after the racing games,
My friends and I have spent these several hours
Watching. Although I do not know your name,
I saw the sun dress half of you with shadow, and I saw
The wind water your eyes as though with tears
Until they flashed like newly-pointed spears.
This afternoon there was a giant daw
Turning above us—though I put no trust
In all these flying omens, being just
A plain man and a warrior, like my friends—
Yet I am mastered by uncommon force
And made to think of you, although it blends
Not with my humor, or the businesses
Of soldiering. I have seen a horse
Moving with more economy, and know
Armor is surer than a girl's promises.
But it is a compelling kind of law
Puts your design before me, even though
I put no faith or fancy in that daw
Turning above us. There's some rigor here,
More than in nature's daily masterpiece
That brings for us, with absolute and clear
Insistence, worms from their midnight soil,
Ungodly honk and trumpeting of geese
In the early morning, and at last the toil
Of soldiering. This is a simple code,
Far simpler than Lycurgus has set down.

The sheep come out of the hills, the sheep come down
When it rains, or gather under a tree,
And in the damp they stink most heartily.
Yet the hills are not so tough but they will yield
Brass for the kitchen, and the soft wet hair
Of the sheep will occupy some fingers. In the bottom fields
The herd's deposit shall assist the spring
Out of the earth and up into the air.
No. There is not a more unbending thing
In nature. It is an order that shall find
You out. There's not a season or a bird can bring
You to my senses or so harness me
To my intention. Let the Helots mind
The barley fields, lest they should see a daw
Turning to perch on some adjacent tree
And fancy it their sovereign ruler. No.
However we are governed, it shall draw
Both of us to its own conclusion, though
I do not even know you by your name.

Discourse Concerning Temptation

Though learned men have been at some dispute
Touching the taste and color, nature, name
And properties of the Original Fruit,
The bees that in midsummer congress swarm
In futile search of apple blossoms can
Testify to a sweetness such as man
Fears in his freezing heart, yet it could warm
Winter away, and redden the cheek with shame.

There was a gentleman of severest taste
Who won from wickedness by consummate strife
A sensibility suitable to his chaste
Formula. He found the world too lavish.
Temptation was his constant, intimate foe,
Constantly to be overcome by force, and so
His formula (fearing lest the world ravish
His senses) applied the rigors of art to life.

But in recurrent dreams saw himself dead,
Mourned by chrysanthemums that walked about,
Each bending over him its massive head
And weeping on him such sweet tender tears
That as each drop spattered upon his limbs
Green plant life blossomed in that place. For hymns
Marking his mean demise, his frigid ears
Perceived the belch of frogs, low and devout.

The problem is not simple. In Guadeloupe
The fer-de-lance displays his ugly trait
Deep in the sweaty undergrowth where droop
Pears of a kind not tasted, where depend
Strange apples, in the shade of *Les Mamelles.*
The place is neither Paradise nor Hell,
But of their divers attributes a blend:
It is man's brief and natural estate.

Samuel Sewall

Samuel Sewall, in a world of wigs,
Flouted opinion in his personal hair;
For foppery he gave not any figs,
But in his right and honor took the air.

Thus in his naked style, though well attired,
He went forth in the city, or paid court
To Madam Winthrop, whom he much admired,
Most godly, but yet liberal with the port.

And all the town admired for two full years
His excellent address, his gifts of fruit,
Her gracious ways and delicate white ears,
And held the course of nature absolute.

But yet she bade him suffer a peruke,
"That One be not distinguished from the All;"
Delivered of herself this stern rebuke
Framed in the resonant language of St. Paul.

"Madam," he answered her, "I have a Friend
Furnishes me with hair out of His strength,
And He requires only I attend
Unto His charity and to its length."

And all the town was witness to his trust:
On Monday he walked out with the Widow Gibbs,
A pious lady of charm and notable bust,
Whose heart beat tolerably beneath her ribs.

On Saturday he wrote proposing marriage,
And closed, imploring that she be not cruel,
"Your favorable answer will oblige,
Madam, your humble servant, Samuel Sewall."

Drinking Song

A toast to that lady over the fireplace
Who wears a snood of pearls. Her eyes are turned
Away from the posterity that loosed
Drunken invaders to the living room,
Toppled the convent bell-tower, and burned
The sniper-ridden outhouses. The face
Of Beatrice d'Este, reproduced
In color, offers a profile to this dark,
Hand-carved interior. High German gloom
Flinches before our boots upon the desk
Where the *Ortsgruppenführer* used to park
His sovereign person. Not a week ago
The women of this house went down among
The stacked-up kindling wood, the picturesque,
Darkening etchings of Vesuvius,
Piled mattresses upon themselves, and shook,
And prayed to God in their guttural native tongue
For mercy, forgiveness, and the death of us.

We are indeed diminished.
                           We are twelve.
But have recaptured a sufficiency
Of France's cognac; and it shall be well,
Given sufficient time, if we can down
Half of it, being as we are, reduced.
Five dead in the pasture, yet they loom
As thirstily as ever. Are recalled
By daring wagers to this living room:
"I'll be around to leak over your grave."

And *Durendal*, my only *Durendal*,
Thou hast preserved me better than a sword;
Rest in the enemy umbrella stand
While that I measure out another drink.
I am beholden to thee, by this hand,
This measuring hand. We are beholden all.

A *Poem for Julia*

Held in her hand of "almost flawless skin"
A small sprig of Sweet William as a badge
Of beauty, and the region of her nose
Seemed to be made so delicate and thin,
Light of the sun might touch the cartilage
With numerous golden tones and hints of rose
If she but turned to the window now to smell
The lilacs and the undulant green lawn,
Trim as a golf course, where a haze revealed
The sheep, distinguished each with a separate bell,
Grazing and moping near the neighbor field
Where all the clover-seeking bees were gone,
But stood in modesty in the full sight
Of Memling, whose accomplished busy hand
Rendered this wimpled lady in such white
Untinted beauty, that she seems to stand
Even as gently to our present gaze
As she had stood there in her breathing days.

Seeing this painting, I am put in mind
Of many a freakish harridan and clown
Who by their native clumsiness or fate
Won for themselves astonishing renown
And stand amongst us even to this date
Since art and history were so inclined:
Here, in a generous Italian scene,
A pimpled, chinless shepherd, whose rough thought
And customary labor lead the ram
Into his sheep for profit and for sport,
Guide their ungainly pleasure with obscene
Mirth at the comedy of sire and dam
Till he has grossly married every ewe—
This shepherd, in a mangy cap of fur,
Stands at the window still regarding her,
That only lady, if the Pope speaks true,
Who with a grace more than we understand
Ate of her portion with a flawless hand.

And once a chattering agent of Pope Paul,
A small, foul-minded clergyman, stood by
To watch the aging Michelangelo
Set his *Last Judgment* on the papal wall,
And muttered thereupon that to his eye
It was a lewd and most indecent show
Of nakedness, not for a sacred place,
Fitted to whorehouse or to public bath;
At which the painter promptly drew his face
Horribly gripped, his face a fist of pain,
Amongst those fixed in God's eternal wrath,
And when the fool made motion to complain
He earned this solemn judgment of the Pope:
"Had art set you on Purgatory's Mount
Then had I done my utmost for your hope,
But Hell's fierce immolation takes no count
Of offices and prayers, for as you know,
From that place *nulla est redemptio.*"

And I recall certain ambassadors,
Cuffed all in ermine and with vests of mail
Who came their way into the town of Prague
Announced by horns, as history tells the tale,
To seek avoidances of future wars
And try the meaning of the Decalogue,
But whispers went about against their names.
And so it happened that a courtier-wit,
Hating their cause with an intemperate might,
Lauded his castle's vantage, and made claims
Upon their courtesy to visit it,
And having brought them to that famous height
To witness the whole streamed and timbered view
Of his ancestral property, and smell
His fine ancestral air, he pushed them through
The open-standing window, whence they fell,
Oh, in a manner worthy to be sung,
Full thirty feet into a pile of dung.

How many poets, with profoundest breath,
Have set their ladies up to spite the worm,
So that pale mistress or high-busted bawd
Could smile and spit into the eye of death
And dance into our midst all fleshed and firm
Despite she was most perishably flawed?
She lasts, but not in her own body's right,
Nor do we love her for her endless poise.
All of her beauty has become a part
Of neighboring beauty, and what could excite
High expectations among hopeful boys
Now leaves her to the nunnery of art.
And yet a searching discipline can keep
That eye still clear, as though in spite of Hell,
So that she seems as innocent as sheep
Where they still graze, denuded of their smell,
Where fool still writhes upon the chapel wall,
A shepherd stares, ambassadors still fall.

Adam and Eve knew such perfection once,
God's finger in the cloud, and on the ground
Nothing but springtime, nothing else at all.
But in our fallen state where the blood hunts
For blood, and rises at the hunting sound,
What do we know of lasting since the fall?
Who has not, in the oil and heat of youth,
Thought of the flourishing of the almond tree,
The grasshopper, and the failing of desire,
And thought his tongue might pierce the secrecy
Of the six-pointed starlight, and might choir
A secret-voweled, unutterable truth?
The heart is ramified with an old force
(Outlingering the blood, out of the sway
Of its own fleshy trap) that finds its source
Deep in the phosphorous waters of the bay,
Or in the wind, or pointing cedar tree,
Or its own ramified complexity.

The Song of the Beasts

(According to ancient Roman law, a man convicted of
parricide was condemned to be flogged, and then sewn
in a sack with a cock, a viper, a dog, and an ape, and
thrown into the sea, or a deep river.)

I am the cock with armored feet,
  Copper feathers and golden eyes;
    The crown of Foolery,
Blood-red and boneless as the jester's crown,
  Betokens my notorious heat,
    Rises upright in vice,
And is my rare, appropriate jewelry.
Water can cleanse, and therefore I must drown.

I am the ape with bestial hair,
  Prehensile feet, and apt for sin,
    A faithful mockery
Of man, his gross and moralizing clown;
  And though he shave his body bare,
    Under the tattered skin
We are one beast beyond all mimicry.
Water can cleanse, and therefore I must drown.

I am the dog of appetites,
  Death passes between my jaws
    And finds no sanctity
In church or grave or laurel-flanked renown:
  Teeth have their old primary rights,
    And disrespectful paws
Deliver bones of their white secrecy.
Water can cleanse, and therefore I must drown.

I am the snake with double tongue,
Incarnate spine of an evil man,
   The legless adversary;
And be he never so brave, he must come down
  Whom my hollow tooth has stung:
    Who as a god began
Must cleave to the ground with Hades' mercenary.
Water can cleanse, and therefore I must drown.

I am the man whose blood must leak
Ungovernable from its home
   Until at last the back,
Torn of the lofty flesh that must come down,
  The nest of furious fang and beak,
    Bear the whole weight of Rome
And all its evil bound into one sack.
Water can cleanse, and therefore I must drown.

Springtime

(From the French of Charles d'Orléans)

The Weather hath put off his mien
Of tearing winde and cold advance,
And beareth new an elegance
Yellow of sun and spritely greene.
Nor bird nor wilde thing to be seen
But shouteth in its own parlance:
"The Weather hath put off his mien
Of tearing winde and cold advance."
And water where it spouteth e'en
Weareth the colors of the dance,
And everyone hath mayde quittance
Of the dark wise of wrath and spleen.
The Weather hath put off his mien.

Songs for the Air
or
Several Attitudes About Breathing

I

We may consider every cloud a lake
Transmogrified, its character unselfed,
At once a whale and a white wedding cake
Bellowed into conspicuous ectoplasm.
It is a lake's ghost that goes voyaging.
And therefore it is fitting we should sing
Of its mild spacious grave, where this phantasm
Glitters like the white porcelain of Delft.

We who shall be so damply put away,
Receiving vigor through dark capillaries,
Must marvel how the delicate decay
Of water makes so elegant a shape.
Air is its earth. This air on which we dine
Bothers the dead lake's body to refine
Its fluidness, and with suggestion merries
The jovial ghost to mimic and to ape.

Faustus, worrying thistle tube and flask,
Dreams of profound Pythagorean changes
That shall contrive for him a living mask.
He does not figure blood thicker than water.
Though a departed pond may promenade
As unicorn or leopard, masquerade
Suits not our tissue, which is rife with manges.
Spittle and mud thicken the human mortar.

II

In the dark belly of a viol, air
Revolved, swirled like a frightened school of perch
Caught in the clever weave of closing nets,
Or, like the spiral steps of minarets,
Whirled round a single dowel of sound, in search
Of the Existence which is named in prayer.

Pinwheels and Ferris wheels of air revolved
To full orchestral pomp, air writhed like blood
In the eccentric bodies of French horns;
Even thus a comic majesty adorns
The Shade of Brandenburg, who rode or stood
On a huge carrousel, till it dissolved.

Or spinning like a Sperry gyroscope,
The air balanced itself on one lean leg,
And, motionless in motion, it bespoke
The poise of an unquestionable Duke,
Till the conductor, brandishing his wig,
Stopped all the air as finally as rope.

III

Lighter than air, Professor Piccard glides
Steadily upward to the stratosphere.
In that unpeopled realm he has no peer.
We have only the thought of him. He strides
The baby-blue continuum, and guides
For the still quarters of his spare retreat.
His feet point down at us like angels' feet.
It is the pure, the matterless abides.

Amid these heavier gases, breath of plants,
Sweat of the sea, belches and coughs and farts,
We bade him Godspeed to the permanent,
Knowing the enterprise for a romance.
Something substantial in our soggy hearts
Anticipated sadly his descent.

IV

If thou must wander in these Woods,
As vagrant as Affection's moods,
Be thou directed, Phyllis, by
Some vigilant Philosophy
That may dissociate thy grief
From seasons simple to the leaf.

Such Learning, though it set thee free
To relish Summer's prodigy,
To love all Ripeness, and to dote
Freely upon the Poet's Oat,
May save thee breathing thy despair
Into this wide incessant Air.

For we must master, if we can,
A Craft particular to Man,
And study through our little Term
To smile at the Ironic Worm
Sequestered at the core of Love
That smiles when it is spoken of.

The Apple that was Venus' prize
Inclines to dazzle human eyes,
And, winning in its golden hue,
Core of the circumscribing Blue,
Seems to enchant the willing Mind
Out of the forces of the wind.

Wherefore I offer thee the Plan
Of a most earnest, gifted man
Who learned "to use my selfe in jest,"
And in this wise might we ingest
The airy Differences that turn
The Thinking Reed or potted Fern.

The newborn Child, held like a Fowl
High by the heels, is taught to howl
For Air and for his mother's Pap
By an invigorating slap;
Thus do our lives at once begin
With an ambiguous Medicine.

And therefore, Girl, when thou dost rove,
Full of uncomplemented Love,
Mourn not to see the Apple fall,
For we are fallen, and may call
Love into being only by
The Shifts of Multiplicity.

Christmas Is Coming

Darkness is for the poor, and thorough cold,
As they go wandering the hills at night,
Gunning for enemies. Winter locks the lake;
The rocks are harder for it. What was grass
Is fossilized and brittle; it can hurt,
Being a torture to the kneeling knee,
And in the general pain of cold, it sticks
Particular pain where crawling is required.

> *Christmas is coming. The goose is getting fat.*
> *Please put a penny in the Old Man's hat.*

Where is the warmth of blood? The enemy
Has ears that can hear clearly in the cold,
Can hear the shattering of fossil grass,
Can hear the stiff cloth rub against itself,
Making a sound. Where is the blood? It lies
Locked in the limbs of some poor animal
In a diaspora of crimson ice.
The skin freezes to metal. One must crawl
Quietly in the dark. Where is the warmth?
The lamb has yielded up its fleece and warmth
And woolly life, but who shall taste of it?
Here on the ground one cannot see the stars.
The lamb is killed. *The goose is getting fat.*
A wind blows steadily against the trees,
And somewhere in the blackness they are black.
Yet crawling one encounters bits of string,
Pieces of foil left by the enemy.
(A rifle takes its temper from the cold.)
Where is the pain? The sense has frozen up,
And fingers cannot recognize the grass,
Cannot distinguish their own character,
Being blind with cold, being stiffened by the cold;
Must find out thistles to remember pain.
Keep to the frozen ground or else be killed.

Yet crawling one encounters in the dark
The frosty carcasses of birds, their feet
And wings all glazed. And still we crawl to learn
Where pain was lost, how to recover pain.
Reach for the brambles, crawl to them and reach,
Clutching for thorns, search carefully to feel
The point of thorns, life's crown, *the Old Man's hat.*
Yet quietly. Do not disturb the brambles.
Winter has taught the air to clarify
All noises, and the enemy can hear
Perfectly in the cold. Nothing but sound
Is known. Where is the warmth and pain?
Christmas is coming. Darkness is for the poor.

> *If you haven't got a penny, a ha'penny will do,*
> *If you haven't got a ha'penny, God bless you.*

Katharsis

The king rose up one morning from his bed
Naming his humors, as was his scholarly style,
And finding above all a viscid bile
Predominated, called for his newlywed,
And with an ax relieved her of her head,
Showing in this that man, however vile,
May through *das ewig-Weibliche* revile
And purge his foulness by her gentle stead.

On that same morning rose up also he
Whose violence had been of lesser scope,
Yet should by stern and eminent decree
Greet his purgation at an end of rope;
He knew no lady, no devoted she
Whose intercession would fulfill the trope.

Imitation

Let men take note of her, touching her shyness,
How grace informs and presses the brocade
Wherein her benefits are whitely stayed,
And think all glittering enterprise, and highness
Of blood or deed were yet in something minus
Lacking the wide approval of her mouth,
And to betoken every man his drouth,
Drink, in her name, all tankards to their dryness.

Wanting her clear perfection, how may tongues
Manifest what no language understands?
Yet as her beauty evermore commands
Even the tanager with tiny lungs
To flush all silence, may she by these songs
Know it was love I looked for at her hands.

The Gardens of the Villa d'Este

This is Italian. Here
Is cause for the undiminished bounce
Of sex, cause for the lark, the animal spirit
To rise, aerated, but not beyond our reach, to spread
Friction upon the air, cause to sing loud for the bed
Of jonquils, the linen bed, and established merit
Of love, and grandly to pronounce
Pleasure without peer.

Goddess, be with me now;
Commend my music to the woods.
There is no garden to the practiced gaze
Half so erotic: here the sixteenth century thew
Rose to its last perfection, this being chiefly due
To the provocative role the water plays.
Tumble and jump, the fountains' moods
Teach the world how.

But, ah, who ever saw
Finer proportion kept. The sum
Of intersecting limbs was something planned.
Ligorio, the laurel! Every turn and quirk
Weaves in this waving green and liquid world to work
Its formula, binding upon the gland,
Even as molecules succumb
To Avogadro's law.

The intricate mesh of trees,
Sagging beneath a lavender snow
Of wisteria, wired by creepers, perfectly knit
A plot to capture alive the migrant, tourist soul
In its corporeal home with all the deft control
And artifice of an Hephaestus' net.
Sunlight and branch rejoice to show
Sudden interstices.

The whole garden inclines
The flesh as water falls, to seek
For depth. Consider the top balustrade,
Where twinned stone harpies, with domed and virgin breasts,
Spurt from their nipples that no pulse or hand has pressed
Clear liquid arcs of benefice and aid
To the chief purpose. They are Greek
Versions of valentines

And spend themselves to fill
The celebrated flumes that skirt
The horseshoe stairs. Triumphant then to a sluice,
With Brownian movement down the giggling water drops
Past haunches, over ledges, out of mouths, and stops
In a still pool, but, by a plumber's ruse,
Rises again to laugh and squirt
At heaven, and is still

Busy descending. White
Ejaculations leap to teach
How fertile are these nozzles; the streams run
Góngora through the garden, channel themselves, and pass
To lily-padded ease, where insubordinate lass
And lad can cool their better parts, where sun
Heats them again to furnace pitch
To prove his law is light.

Marble the fish that puke
Eternally, marble the lips
Of gushing naiads, pleased to ridicule
Adonis, marble himself, and larger than life-sized,
Untouched by Venus, posthumously circumcised
Patron of Purity; and any fool
Who feels no flooding at the hips
These spendthrift stones rebuke.

It was in such a place
  That Mozart's Figaro contrived
 The totally expected. This is none
Of your French topiary, geometric works,
Based on God's rational, wrist-watch universe; here lurks
  The wood louse, the night crawler, the homespun
    Spider; here are they born and wived
      And bedded, by God's grace.

      Actually, it is real
  The way the world is real: the horse
 Must turn against the wind, and the deer feed
Against the wind, and finally the garden must allow
For the recalcitrant; a style can teach us how
  To know the world in little where the weed
    Has license, where by dint of force
      D'Estes have set their seal.

      Their spirit entertains.
  And we are honorable guests
 Come by imagination, come by night,
Hearing in the velure of darkness impish strings
Mincing Tartini, hearing the hidden whisperings:
  "*Carissima*, the moon gives too much light,"
    Though by its shining it invests
      Her bodice with such gains

      As show their shadowed worth
  Deep in the cleavage. Lanterns, lamps
 Of pumpkin-colored paper dwell upon
The implications of the skin-tight silk, allude
Directly to the body; under the subdued
  Report of corks, whisperings, the *chaconne*,
    Boisterous water runs its ramps
      Out, to the end of mirth.

37

Accommodating plants
Give umbrage where the lovers delve
Deeply for love, give way to their delight,
As Pliny's pregnant mouse, bearing unborn within her
Lewd sons and pregnant daughters, hears the adept beginner:
"*Cor mio,* your supports are much too tight,"
While overhead the stars resolve
Every extravagance.

Tomorrow, before dawn,
Gardeners will come to resurrect
Downtrodden iris, dispose of broken glass,
Return the diamond earrings to the villa, but
As for the moss upon the statue's shoulder, not
To defeat its green invasion, but to pass
Over the liberal effect
Caprice and cunning spawn.

For thus it was designed:
Controlled disorder at the heart
Of everything, the paradox, the old
Oxymoronic itch to set the formal strictures
Within a natural context, where the tension lectures
Us on our mortal state, and by controlled
Disorder, labors to keep art
From being too refined.

Susan, it had been once
My hope to see this place with you,
See it as in the hour of thoughtless youth.
For age mocks all diversity, its genesis,
And whispers to the heart, "*Cor mio,* beyond all this
Lies the unchangeable and abstract truth,"
Claims of the grass, it is not true,
And makes our youth its dunce.

Therefore, some later day
Recall these words, let them be read
Between us, let them signify that here
Are more than formulas, that age sees no more clearly
For its poor eyesight, and philosophy grows surly,
That falling water and the blood's career
Lead down the garden path to bed
And win us both to May.

Seascape with Figures

FOR IVAN MAJDRAKOFF

Lean, fluted, Corinthian columns of air
Rose in the pipes and whistles of that ship
For our departure, Ivan. Deep is the sea,
And vile her salty purpose, but we rode
Grand in the cordial harbor to the gree
Of celebrating gulls, where tugboats towed
Our bulk before that sexless, metal She
Molded in France. The stained and vacant stare
Of Liberty on the waters, book on hip,
Boded us bad, looked sorely on our trip,
Augured a freedom difficult to bear;
But we went stately just as the tide flowed.

Triremes of Greece, like sea-borne centipedes,
Left circled footprints where the oarsmen dipped
Their blades in rhythm to the whipper's pace,
But churned no beauty like our boiling wake:
The marble sea sprouting with Queen Anne's Lace.
Under that filigree, propellers rake
Atlantic's flesh to get us to our place.
Turn of the screw in time and water speeds
The French hairdresser home, flutters the gripped
Hearts of the trim-coifed nuns in bevy shipped
To that poor quarter where their host still bleeds,
To Patrick's Ireland, green and without snake.

O we were propped, Ivan, against all pain
By dint of hope, by ample *Schwärmerei,*
By that salt smell and savor, as the birds
Flapped their absurd applause to our escape.
It is the bar, it is the drink that girds;
Fluid the cause *finalis* of the grape.
Nothing in transit need be done by thirds.
No dolphin leaps unmounted in that main
If but imagination leap and try
The volume of our round and clement sky.
Then fluent as the sea or drink, the brain
Floats handsomely upon the liquid scape.

But four days out, out of the sight of Her,
The sea went black with wrath and there were groans
More sounding than the cold Aeolian gale
Plucked in our rigging. Then we thought of shore.
Being both man and fish, both flesh and scale,
Triton was fitted better for this war.
The nuns went all devoutly to the rail.
Our ship danced like a drunken Lucifer
Fathoms above the treasury of bones
That whiten for the pearls of Davy Jones,
Pranced like a giddy fiend, and all the whir
Of water, his chaotic metaphor.

What, then, is freedom? Merely to be free
Is nothing. On the seventh day the lights
Of France's harbor flecked the orchid gloom
Of early morning, doubled again their glow
Upon the Channel waters. Raging spume
Departed from us. On the dock a row
Of stevedores observed the sound and fume
Rise from our whistles in a fleur-de-lis.
But yet the logic of the heart delights
In its first figure, nor will hazard flights
Till we assail again such liberty
Late in September as the tide shall flow.

A Deep Breath at Dawn

Morning has come at last. The rational light
Discovers even the humblest thing that yearns
For heaven; from its scaled and shadeless height,
Figures its difficult way among the ferns,
Nests in the trees, and is ambitious to warm
The chilled vein, and to light the spider's thread
With modulations hastening to a storm
Of the full spectrum, rushing from red to red.
I have watched its refinements since the dawn,
When, at the birdcall, all the ghosts were gone.

The wolf, the fig tree, and the woodpecker
Were sacred once to Undertaker Mars;
Honor was done in Rome to that home-wrecker
Whose armor and whose ancient, toughened scars
Made dance the very meat of Venus' heart,
And hot her ichor, and immense her eyes,
Till his rough ways and her invincible art
Locked and laid low their shining, tangled thighs.
My garden yields his fig tree, even now
Bearing heraldic fruit at every bough.

Someone I have not seen for six full years
Might pass this garden through, and might pass by
The oleander bush, the bitter pears
Unfinished by the sun, with only an eye
For the sun-speckled shade of the fig tree,
And shelter in its gloom, and raise his hand
For tribute and for nourishment (for he
Was once entirely at the god's command)
But that his nature, being all undone,
Cannot abide the clarity of the sun.

Morning deceived him those six years ago.
Morning swam in the pasture, being all green
And yellow, and the swallow coiled in slow
Passage of dials and spires above the scene
Cluttered with dandelions, near the fence
Where the hens strutted redheaded and wreathed
With dark, imponderable chicken sense,
Hardly two hundred yards from where he breathed,
And where, from their declamatory roosts,
The cocks cried brazenly against all ghosts.

Warmth in the milling air, the warmth of blood;
The dampness of the earth; the forest floor
Of fallen needles, the dried and creviced mud,
Lay matted and caked with sunlight, and the war
Seemed elsewhere; light impeccable, unmixed,
Made accurate the swallow's traveling print
Over the pasture, till he saw it fixed
Perfectly on a little patch of mint.
And he could feel in his body, driven home,
The wild tooth of the wolf that suckled Rome.

What if he came and stood beside my tree,
A poor, transparent thing with nothing to do,
His chest showing a jagged vacancy
Through which I might admire the distant view?
My house is solid, and the windows house
In their fine membranes the gelatinous light,
But darkness follows, and the dark allows
Obscure hints of a tapping sound at night.
And yet it may be merely that I dream
A woodpecker attacks the attic beam.

It is as well the light keeps him away;
We should have little to say in days like these,
Although once friends. We should have little to say,
But that there will be much planting of fig trees,
And Venus shall be clad in the prim leaf,
And turn a solitary. And her god, forgot,
Cast by that emblem out, shall spend his grief
Upon us. In that day the fruit shall rot
Unharvested. Then shall the sullen god
Perform his mindless fury in our blood.

Divination by a Cat

Fence walker, balancer, your devil-may-care
Astounds the workman teetering on his girder
Whom gravity and the pavement want to murder,
    But with eight lives to spare
Who would lack courage? From his jungle-gym
He lowers, thin as a hair, the strand of fear
To plumb the seventy stories under him,
    And for his firm intent
The spirit level of the inner ear
    Is his chief instrument.

But you are classic, striking the S-curve
In a half-gainer from some eminence,
And with Athenian equipoise and sense
    To qualify your nerve,
End up unerringly upon your feet.
O this is Greek to all of us. I dare
Construe your figure for our human fate,
    And like the Pythoness
Decoding viscera, anoint the air
    With emblematic guess.

You are the lesser Tiger, yet the night
Blazes with the combustion of your eye,
And we, in our imperfect symmetry,
    Combining double sight,
Can see mirrored in your chatoyant gaze
Our fire, slight, diminished. If the first
Intensity return of that white blaze
    To run our bodies through,
Might it not burn us? If the fire burst,
    Will it not barbecue?

Cat, you are meat for study. All our youth
Shall vanish, like your literary kin,
Dwindle into a disembodied grin;
    And if we want the truth,
Why, we must cram for it, gather your drift,
Like that odd family trudging from St. Ives.
Be Plutarch to our ignorance; your gift
    Compares Athens to Rome,
And the collected tails of all your lives
    Shall drive the moral home.

A Roman Holiday

I write from Rome. Last year, the Holy Year,
The flock was belled, and pilgrims came to see
How milkweed mocked the buried engineer,
Wedging between his marble works, where free
And famished went the lions forth to tear
A living meal from the offending knee,
And where, on pagan ground, turned to our good,
Santa Maria sopra Minerva stood.

And came to see where Caesar Augustus turned
Brick into marble, thus to celebrate
Apollo's Peace, that lately had been learned,
And where the Rock that bears the Church's weight,
Crucified Peter, raised his eyes and yearned
For final sight of heavenly estate,
But saw ungainly huge above his head
Our stony base to which the flesh is wed.

And see the wealthy, terraced Palatine,
Where once the unknown god or goddess ruled
In mystery and silence, whose divine
Name has been lost or hidden from the fooled,
Daydreaming employee who guards the shrine
And has forgotten how men have been schooled
To hide the Hebrew Vowels, that craft or sin
Might not pronounce their sacred origin.

And has forgot that on the temple floor
Once was a Vestal Virgin overcome
Even by muscle of the god of war,
And ran full of unearthly passion home,
Being made divinity's elected whore
And fertile with the twins that founded Rome.
Columns are down. Unknown the ruined face
Of travertine, found in a swampy place.

Yet there was wisdom even then that said,
Nothing endures at last but only One;
Sands shift in the wind, petals are shed,
Eternal cities also are undone;
Informed the living and the pious dead
That there is no new thing under the sun,
Nor can the best ambition come to good
When it is founded on a brother's blood.

I write from Rome. It is late afternoon
Nearing the Christmas season. Blooded light
Floods through the Colosseum, where platoon
And phalanx of the Lord slaved for the might
Of Titus' pleasure. Blood repeats its tune
Loudly against my eardrums as I write,
And recollects what they were made to pay
Who out of worship put their swords away.

The bells declare it. "Crime is at the base,"
Rings in the belfry where the blood is choired.
Crime stares from the unknown, ruined face,
And the cold wind, endless and wrath-inspired,
Cries out for judgment in a swampy place
As darkness claims the trees. "Blood is required,
And it shall fall," below the Seven Hills
The blood of Remus whispers out of wells.

Speech

I have discouraged that in me
Wherewith I most advance:
Too easy eloquence of speech,
A sailing present tense;
Fearing that if the mind conspires
Mainly to please the lip,
Time will point out the flattery,
The language will not grip.

But when the talker's sleight of tongue
Required us to laugh,
Proving the agile, unrehearsed,
Triumphantly pays off,
Then praise was for a kind of art
Whereof there is no school;
There the unlettered instinct rides
In all its bodily skill.

At the Frick

Before a grotto of blue-tinted rock
Master Bellini has set down St. Francis.
A light split through the Apennines to lock,
Counter, and splice man's painful doubleness,
Else he could weakly couple at the belt
His kite-mind to his cloven nether parts
That seek to dance their independent dances.
The sudden light descending came to bless
His hands and feet with blisters, and to melt
With loving that most malleable of hearts.

Birds in the trees his chronicle recite:
How that God made of him a living net
To catch all graces, yet to let through light.
Fisher of birds and lepers, lost in thought,
Darkly emblazoned, where the oblivious mule
Champs at the grasses and the sunset rusts
The hilltop fortress, where the painter set
Heron and rabbit, it was here he caught
Holiness that came swimming like a school
Of silver fishes to outflash his lusts.

Now I have seen those mountains, and have seen
The fawn go frozen on the road with fear
Of the careening autobus, the sheen
Of its dilated eyes flash in its head
Like glass reflectors, and have seen the trees
As green as ever where their branches thresh
The warm Italian winds of one more year
Since that great instant. The painter's dead
Who brought the Doge and nobles to the knees
Of the wind's Brother Francis in the flesh.

A Valentine

February; the untented blizzard treads
Against us, and again the poor must heel
Into the weather with embattled heads.
   Which of us shall not feel
The pinch of winter, and the punishment
Of an unfeeling heaven? Blow your thumb,
And though your breath be clear and innocent
   The finger shall go numb.
Although our little warmth cannot be spared
Lightly to challenge with uncovered parts
Such chilling force, this day has been declared
   The festival of hearts.

My darling, what shall you have to mark this day?
What testimony against this bitter air
That loves no one at all, and seems to say,
   "O ye who greatly dare,
I will cast back into your chattering teeth
All vows and pledges. Go, look to the poor.
Shall not myself possess all here beneath?
   And shall ye then endure?"
What shall you have? A crimson cardboard heart,
Fringed with a paper doily, weakly pinned
With the cheap metal foil of Cupid's dart,
   To bear against this wind?

For my own heart, I fear, no skill commends
Its services to you; if it maintain
Clemency where this weather most offends,
    Surely the frost will gain
Upon its essence, and will execute
Its little bravery of cardinal red.
It has only its folly to refute
    All that the wind has said;
And is not much deserving at your hands,
But that it has been tried by the full sore
Of the air's worst extremity, and stands
    Naked before your door.

Alceste in the Wilderness

Non, je ne puis souffrir cette lâche méthode
Qu'affectent la plupart de vos gens à la mode . . .

MOLIERE: Le Misanthrope

Evening is clogged with gnats as the light fails,
And branches bloom with gold and copper screams
Of birds with figured and sought-after tails
To plume a lady's gear; the motet wails
Through Africa upon dissimilar themes.

A little snuffbox whereon Daphnis sings
In pale enamels, touching love's defeat,
Calls up the color of her underthings
And plays upon the taut memorial strings,
Trailing her laces down into this heat.

One day he found, topped with a smutty grin,
The small corpse of a monkey, partly eaten.
Force of the sun had split the bluish skin,
Which, by their questioning and entering in,
A swarm of bees had been concerned to sweeten.

He could distill no essence out of this.
That yellow majesty and molten light
Should bless this carcass with a sticky kiss
Argued a brute and filthy emphasis.
The half-moons of the fingernails were white,

And where the nostrils opened on the skies,
Issuing to the sinus, where the ant
Crawled swiftly down to undermine the eyes
Of cloudy aspic, nothing could disguise
How terribly the thing looked like Philinte.

Will-o'-the-wisp, on the scum-laden water,
Burns in the night, a gaseous deceiver,
In the pale shade of France's foremost daughter.
Heat gives his thinking cavity no quarter,
For he is burning with the monkey's fever.

Before the bees have diagrammed their comb
Within the skull, before summer has cracked
The back of Daphnis, naked, polychrome,
Versailles shall see the tempered exile home,
Peruked and stately for the final act.

Harangue

While, like a holy man, you kissed the sores
On the long corpus of society,
Divining filthy dreams it had in life,
The unbecoming seepings of its pores
Gathering meaning for you; while your knife
Picked at the chambers of the soul, the liver,
And you made notes to document the cluster
Of tumors breeding to satiety,
With all bravado I could ably muster
I went for a sunny walk beside the river.

I can report no news about the birds.
They are as ignorant as ever, sing
In thoroughgoing boneheaded defiance
Of all your findings. At a loss for words,
They none the less repudiate your science.
I have not the presumption to defend
Such arrant warbling. My embarrassed logic
Scored not at all against the treble ring
Of music so unsuited to the tragic.
They seemed to have no inkling of their end.

Bird-witted? Doubtless, but their noisy creed
Was seconded by inarticulate trees
Whose wooden quiddity, erect and pliant,
Sprouting luxurious beyond all need,
Was by excess thus equally defiant,
And all my thought, though diligent and tidy,
Could not yet disestablish such a green
Outburst. My walk was pleasant as you please,
Yet, puzzling what I have heard and seen,
I have come back to interrupt your study.

Let us engage this difficulty. Trees
Commit their rage of brilliance to the span
Of summer, and their tenant minstrelsy
Thins in the winter till the season freeze
River to stopping, petrify the tree,
Throttle its small musicians, set the leaf
Flying insanely in its paper age
To a berserk and violent death. Yet man,
Outliving both the summer and its rage,
Numbers his days and knows them to be brief.

"Man," as you often quote, "created death,"
And tell me of a man so keenly tried
By the unaging passions in his veins
He prayed for comfort with his aging breath,
Praying to be delivered from the pains
That bind the body by a narrow thong
To its mortality. And yet the flesh
Is nothing but the substance that defied
All reasoning; it is the green excess
That tops the trees, and of the birds their song.

What shall we do with our "creation?" Germs
Of metaphysics have their breeding here.
Terror and hope are hatched. It seems the dead,
Though provender for the man-eating worms,
Baffle us at the table and in bed
With stark arithmetic and perfect reason.
Therefore we riddle sadly on the tree,
Figure in stars the story of our year.
Not for themselves but for our mystery
We watch the swift migrations of the season.

When Leeuwenhoek, with clear courageous eye,
Peered gamely through his masterpiece of quartz,
Witnessing tiny life, to his astound,
He saw death no more certainly than I
Who, in the summertime, upon the ground,
Have studied nature through a rifle sight.
Caught in this reticle, the nearly dead
Display an animation that distorts.
The crossing filaments of spider's thread
Have drawn and quartered heroes at their height.

Granted, there's reason for our reasoning.
The tree becomes the instrument of passion;
The bird is Death, the Violated Lady,
And that high ditty that we hear her sing
Calls us away, whether or not we're ready.
Yet there is substance here beyond our talk,
Stuff that defies the cynical romancer
To whittle to his fantasy and fashion,
And while you meditate upon your answer
I shall go back to the river for a walk.

Hallowe'en

Tonight our streets are filled
With beardless pirates and their high-heeled wives
Who own no maps of treasure and have killed
Nobody with their aimless wooden knives;
They cry us charity for their cups of tin.
    Tonight their plea is styled
With signs of poison and the threat of crones,
While from behind a soap-scrawled windowpane,
A pumpkin with a candle for a brain
    Flashes its hacked-out grin
At Jolly Roger, ensign of the child
Who stalks the street, superfluous of bones.

One time the children came
Souling with little songs for all the dead,
Soliciting in Mystery's full name
Apples and cakes and pies, for it was said
A hermit raised a trapdoor and was shown
    Where purgatory burned,
Whistled and hurt; he heard the demons yell
Against the monks of Cluny for their prayers
That lifted cripples up the spiraled stairs.
    And singing made it known:
To do grace to the dead, lest they returned,
Apples were prayers and giving was a spell.

And singers have this right,
For hunger haunts the gut, but not for bread;
The troubled presence that returns this night,
When all the air is crowded with the dead,
Shivers for lack of body, and is claim
    To the community
Of the mad Prince disguised in seven ways,
The Riddling Knight who challenges our sleep,
The starving Goblin and the Hag who keep
    (To their perpetual blame)
Poor Tom o' Bedlam from his sanity,
And sent an English king into his craze.

    All of our enemies
Move through this night with polished, skinless jaws,
And kiss the daft ones into their disease,
Take from the poor, and are themselves the cause
That ghosts return upon us to be fed.
    Hearing the Death's Head cry,
"O hunger, hunger," shall I offer salt?
The pumpkin grins with idiotic mirth,
Laughs at the child whose bones were crossed at birth,
    Who moves among these dead,
Hungry for bread and salt, and ripe to die,
And likely to come, begging, from the vault.

Spring for Thomas Hardy

These are the weathers Hardy praised
    In his best tongue;
When spring comes uttered forth unphrased,
    Straight from the lung;
And the deep, bearded roots unfreeze,
And soapsuds shake in the flimsy breeze,
And girls find cause to show their knees,
And a warm rain riddles the alders: these
    He'd chiefly sung.

As he was one whose leaning made
    Note of such things,
I read him still in the primest blade
    The weather brings;
And I doubt not, as the snails appear,
And the light is blond as a glass of beer,
When the songbird ravishes every ear
It is for someone who cannot hear
    He chiefly sings.

A Lesson from the Master

These fruits are lovely, and the minuets
Extremely danceable. That there were shepherds here
I have no doubt at all: pots have been found
Suggesting pastoral life. But when the heart
Beats at a long remove from all these things
(Remembering how the murderous virgins bit
The bay leaf to perfect their lust, what birds
Dipped omens of bad weather to the fleet,
The taste and hue of the specific pear)
Then thought flows into vistas and is lost.
These trophies demand trophies for themselves
And bear away the blood, bear it away.
Passion belongs in the forsaken wrist;
Knowing no past, it is immediate
Though night will come as easily tonight
As ever before, crowding with lavenders
The scenes of our misgivings, just as grave
As ever before. Fruit is no help for this.
No consolation. Only a reproof.

Behind those alders walks the Passionate Man;
His arms we imagine sleeved in summer air,
Modeled by shifting light. He goes unseen.
The birds obscure him with spontaneous trills
Shaped by the leaves and passages of light.
Their songs are branched and unaccountable.
Hair-footed water spiders skate the pond
And fruit dangles above. He goes unseen.
It is because his heart sings to itself
The birds ignore him, and their public song,
Shaped by the leaves and passages of light,
Strikes us as branched and unaccountable.
Yet, if the heart were known . . . I say these things
Not without difficulty. Death is always here,
And birth, and sickness; also the accident
Of Fate bringing together four warm legs

(Although her eyes are blear, although his feet
Corrupt the world with odor). There is prayer,
And hope of Heaven after all. The Child,
The Winter Child was hammered to the tree,
Dangled above like fruit; when He looked down
He saw there in that crowd the Passionate Man.
We have report of that occasion. Now
The Passionate Man has learned in his fell heart
There is one Passion that is serious.
And we who walk below, eying the fruit,
Sniffing the air for spring, and flipping coins,
Are given to extravagance in love,
In battle, and in sorrow. This is right.
Our ways are human and ridiculous,
Familiar to the heart. We know the tree
By the compassionate fruit that it has borne;
And blessed be Adam for his thievery,
The loot being restored by Heaven's grace,
The fruit being renewed at every spring.
Can we not easily laugh, then, and drink beer,
Or curse the weather and attend to work,
Loving those whom we love, letting the blood,
Vivace, run its course, for that we are
Surely the children of the Passionate Man?

Now in these poems—the well-balanced cat,
This one of pliant clouds, this weeping skull,
The saint reeling with godliness—I hear
A voice behind these words, behind the green
Proliferation of the sparrow's home,
Behind the air. The speaker goes unseen.
Yet I would know him, if the heart were known.
Close with this world; incorporate this voice.
Lovers cannot forever stand apart,
Eying each other's flanks, and whistling tunes
To cool their lips, choosing their thoughts to build
A zodiacal context for their act.
Bring them to bed. Let her embarrassment

Be clear as her desire. Let his dim thought
Gather as weakly as the powdered light
The moon casts on the bedsheets and the floor
Gathers along the cool unpeopled streets,
Defining crumpled newspapers that lie,
Littered with filth, beside the pavement steps
When browns and grays are gathered from their gloom.

God give us bread; we'll make the circuses.